D1169948

THE OLD MAN AND THE SEA

Ernest Hemingway

SPARK PUBLISHING

© 2002, 2007 by Spark Publishing

All rights reserved. No part of this publication may be reproduced, stored in a
retrieval system, or transmitted, in any form or by any means, electronic, mechanical,
photocopying, recording, or otherwise, without prior written permission from the
publisher.

SPARKNOTES is a registered trademark of SparkNotes LLC

Spark Publishing
A Division of Barnes & Noble
120 Fifth Avenue
New York, NY 10011
www.sparknotes.com

ISBN-13: 978-1-4114-0377-2
ISBN-10: 1-4114-0377-0

Please submit changes or report errors to www.sparknotes.com/errors.

Printed in the United States.

10 9 8 7 6 5 4

CONTENTS

CONTEXT

ERNEST HEMINGWAY WAS BORN in Oak Park, Illinois, in 1899, the son of a doctor and a music teacher. He began his writing career as a reporter for the Kansas City *Star*. At age eighteen, he volunteered to serve as a Red Cross ambulance driver in World War I and was sent to Italy, where he was badly injured by shrapnel. Hemingway later fictionalized his experience in Italy in what some consider his greatest novel, *A Farewell to Arms*. In 1921, Hemingway moved to Paris, where he served as a correspondent for the Toronto *Daily Star*. In Paris, he fell in with a group of American and English expatriate writers that included F. Scott Fitzgerald, Ezra Pound, Gertrude Stein, and Ford Madox Ford. In the early 1920s, Hemingway began to achieve fame as a chronicler of the disaffection felt by many American youth after World War I—a generation of youth whom Stein memorably dubbed the "Lost Generation." His novels *The Sun Also Rises* (1926) and *A Farewell to Arms* (1929) established him as a dominant literary voice of his time. His spare, charged style of writing was revolutionary at the time and would be imitated, for better or for worse, by generations of young writers to come.

After leaving Paris, Hemingway wrote on bullfighting, published short stories and articles, covered the Spanish Civil War as a journalist, and published his best-selling novel, *For Whom the Bell Tolls* (1940). These pieces helped Hemingway build up the mythic breed of masculinity for which he wished to be known. His work and his life revolved around big-game hunting, fishing, boxing, and bullfighting, endeavors that he tried to master as seriously as he did writing. In the 1930s, Hemingway lived in Key West, Florida, and later in Cuba, and his years of experience fishing the Gulf Stream and the Caribbean provided an essential background for the vivid descriptions of the fisherman's craft in *The Old Man and the Sea*. In 1936, he wrote a piece for *Esquire* about a Cuban fisherman who was dragged out to sea by a great marlin, a game fish that typically weighs hundreds of pounds. Sharks had destroyed the fisherman's catch by the time he was found half-delirious by other fishermen. This story seems an obvious seed for the tale of Santiago in *The Old Man and the Sea*.

A great fan of baseball, Hemingway liked to talk in the sport's lingo, and by 1952, he badly "needed a win." His novel *Across the River and Into the Trees,* published in 1950, was a disaster. It was his first novel in ten years, and he had claimed to friends that it was his best yet. Critics, however, disagreed and called the work the worst thing Hemingway had ever written. Many readers claimed it read like a parody of Hemingway. The control and precision of his earlier prose seemed to be lost beyond recovery.

The huge success of *The Old Man and the Sea,* published in 1952, was a much-needed vindication. The novella won the 1953 Pulitzer Prize for Fiction, and it likely cinched the Nobel Prize for Hemingway in 1954, as it was cited for particular recognition by the Nobel Academy. It was the last novel published in his lifetime.

Although the novella helped to regenerate Hemingway's wilting career, it has since been met by divided critical opinion. While some critics have praised *The Old Man and the Sea* as a new classic that takes its place among such established American works as William Faulkner's short story "The Bear" and Herman Melville's *Moby-Dick,* others have attacked the story as "imitation Hemingway" and find fault with the author's departure from the uncompromising realism with which he made his name.

Because Hemingway was a writer who always relied heavily on autobiographical sources, some critics, not surprisingly, eventually decided that the novella served as a thinly veiled attack upon them. According to this reading, Hemingway was the old master at the end of his career being torn apart by—but ultimately triumphing over—critics on a feeding frenzy. But this reading ultimately reduces *The Old Man and the Sea* to little more than an act of literary revenge. The more compelling interpretation asserts that the novella is a parable about life itself, in particular man's struggle for triumph in a world that seems designed to destroy him.

Despite the soberly life-affirming tone of the novella, Hemingway was, at the end of his life, more and more prone to debilitating bouts of depression. He committed suicide in 1961 in Ketchum, Idaho.

Plot Overview

T HE OLD MAN AND THE SEA is the story of an epic struggle between an old, seasoned fisherman and the greatest catch of his life. For eighty-four days, Santiago, an aged Cuban fisherman, has set out to sea and returned empty-handed. So conspicuously unlucky is he that the parents of his young, devoted apprentice and friend, Manolin, have forced the boy to leave the old man in order to fish in a more prosperous boat. Nevertheless, the boy continues to care for the old man upon his return each night. He helps the old man tote his gear to his ramshackle hut, secures food for him, and discusses the latest developments in American baseball, especially the trials of the old man's hero, Joe DiMaggio. Santiago is confident that his unproductive streak will soon come to an end, and he resolves to sail out farther than usual the following day.

On the eighty-fifth day of his unlucky streak, Santiago does as promised, sailing his skiff far beyond the island's shallow coastal waters and venturing into the Gulf Stream. He prepares his lines and drops them. At noon, a big fish, which he knows is a marlin, takes the bait that Santiago has placed one hundred fathoms deep in the waters. The old man expertly hooks the fish, but he cannot pull it in. Instead, the fish begins to pull the boat.

Unable to tie the line fast to the boat for fear the fish would snap a taut line, the old man bears the strain of the line with his shoulders, back, and hands, ready to give slack should the marlin make a run. The fish pulls the boat all through the day, through the night, through another day, and through another night. It swims steadily northwest until at last it tires and swims east with the current. The entire time, Santiago endures constant pain from the fishing line. Whenever the fish lunges, leaps, or makes a dash for freedom, the cord cuts Santiago badly. Although wounded and weary, the old man feels a deep empathy and admiration for the marlin, his brother in suffering, strength, and resolve.

On the third day the fish tires, and Santiago, sleep-deprived, aching, and nearly delirious, manages to pull the marlin in close enough to kill it with a harpoon thrust. Dead beside the skiff, the marlin is the largest Santiago has ever seen. He lashes it to his boat, raises the small mast, and sets sail for home. While Santiago is excited by the price that the marlin will bring at market, he is more concerned that the people who will eat the fish are unworthy of its greatness.

As Santiago sails on with the fish, the marlin's blood leaves a trail in the water and attracts sharks. The first to attack is a great mako shark, which Santiago manages to slay with the harpoon. In the struggle, the old man loses the harpoon and lengths of valuable rope, which leaves him vulnerable to other shark attacks. The old man fights off the successive vicious predators as best he can, stabbing at them with a crude spear he makes by lashing a knife to an oar, and even clubbing them with the boat's tiller. Although he kills several sharks, more and more appear, and by the time night falls, Santiago's continued fight against the scavengers is useless. They devour the marlin's precious meat, leaving only skeleton, head, and tail. Santiago chastises himself for going "out too far," and for sacrificing his great and worthy opponent. He arrives home before daybreak, stumbles back to his shack, and sleeps very deeply.

The next morning, a crowd of amazed fishermen gathers around the skeletal carcass of the fish, which is still lashed to the boat. Knowing nothing of the old man's struggle, tourists at a nearby café observe the remains of the giant marlin and mistake it for a shark. Manolin, who has been worried sick over the old man's absence, is moved to tears when he finds Santiago safe in his bed. The boy fetches the old man some coffee and the daily papers with the baseball scores, and watches him sleep. When the old man wakes, the two agree to fish as partners once more. The old man returns to sleep and dreams his usual dream of lions at play on the beaches of Africa.

CHARACTER LIST

Santiago   The old man of the novella's title, Santiago is a Cuban fisherman who has had an extended run of bad luck. Despite his expertise, he has been unable to catch a fish for eighty-four days. He is humble, yet exhibits a justified pride in his abilities. His knowledge of the sea and its creatures, and of his craft, is unparalleled and helps him preserve a sense of hope regardless of circumstance. Throughout his life, Santiago has been presented with contests to test his strength and endurance. The marlin with which he struggles for three days represents his greatest challenge. Paradoxically, although Santiago ultimately loses the fish, the marlin is also his greatest victory.

The marlin   Santiago hooks the marlin, which we learn at the end of the novella measures eighteen feet, on the first afternoon of his fishing expedition. Because of the marlin's great size, Santiago is unable to pull the fish in, and the two become engaged in a kind of tug-of-war that often seems more like an alliance than a struggle. The fishing line serves as a symbol of the fraternal connection Santiago feels with the fish. When the captured marlin is later destroyed by sharks, Santiago feels destroyed as well. Like Santiago, the marlin is implicitly compared to Christ.

Manolin   A boy presumably in his adolescence, Manolin is Santiago's apprentice and devoted attendant. The old man first took him out on a boat when he was merely five years old. Due to Santiago's recent bad luck, Manolin's parents have forced the boy to go out on a different fishing boat. Manolin, however, still cares deeply for the old man, to whom he continues to look as a mentor. His love for Santiago is unmistakable as the two discuss baseball and as the young boy recruits help from villagers to improve the old man's impoverished conditions.

Joe DiMaggio Although DiMaggio never appears in the novel, he plays a significant role nonetheless. Santiago worships him as a model of strength and commitment, and his thoughts turn toward DiMaggio whenever he needs to reassure himself of his own strength. Despite a painful bone spur that might have crippled another player, DiMaggio went on to secure a triumphant career. He was a center fielder for the New York Yankees from 1936 to 1951, and is often considered the best all-around player ever at that position.

Perico Perico, the reader assumes, owns the bodega in Santiago's village. He never appears in the novel, but he serves an important role in the fisherman's life by providing him with newspapers that report the baseball scores. This act establishes him as a kind man who helps the aging Santiago.

Martin Like Perico, Martin, a café owner in Santiago's village, does not appear in the story. The reader learns of him through Manolin, who often goes to Martin for Santiago's supper. As the old man says, Martin is a man of frequent kindness who deserves to be repaid.

ANALYSIS OF MAJOR CHARACTERS

SANTIAGO

Santiago suffers terribly throughout *The Old Man and the Sea*. In the opening pages of the book, he has gone eighty-four days without catching a fish and has become the laughingstock of his small village. He then endures a long and grueling struggle with the marlin only to see his trophy catch destroyed by sharks. Yet, the destruction enables the old man to undergo a remarkable transformation, and he wrests triumph and renewed life from his seeming defeat. After all, Santiago is an old man whose physical existence is almost over, but the reader is assured that Santiago will persist through Manolin, who, like a disciple, awaits the old man's teachings and will make use of those lessons long after his teacher has died. Thus, Santiago manages, perhaps, the most miraculous feat of all: he finds a way to prolong his life after death.

Santiago's commitment to sailing out farther than any fisherman has before, to where the big fish promise to be, testifies to the depth of his pride. Yet, it also shows his determination to change his luck. Later, after the sharks have destroyed his prize marlin, Santiago chastises himself for his hubris (exaggerated pride), claiming that it has ruined both the marlin and himself. True as this might be, it is only half the picture, for Santiago's pride also enables him to achieve his most true and complete self. Furthermore, it helps him earn the deeper respect of the village fishermen and secures him the prized companionship of the boy—he knows that he will never have to endure such an epic struggle again.

Santiago's pride is what enables him to endure, and it is perhaps endurance that matters most in Hemingway's conception of the world—a world in which death and destruction, as part of the natural order of things, are unavoidable. Hemingway seems to believe that there are only two options: defeat or endurance until destruction; Santiago clearly chooses the latter. His stoic determination is mythic, nearly Christ-like in proportion. For three days, he holds fast to the line that links him to the fish, even though it cuts deeply into his palms, causes a crippling cramp in his left hand, and ruins his back. This physical pain allows Santiago to forge a connection with the marlin that goes beyond the literal link of the line: his bodily aches attest to the fact that he is well matched, that the fish is a worthy opponent, and that he himself, because he is able to fight so hard, is a worthy fisherman. This connectedness to the world around him eventually elevates Santiago beyond what would otherwise be his defeat. Like Christ, to whom Santiago is unashamedly compared at the end of the novella, the old man's physical suffering leads to a more significant spiritual triumph.

MANOLIN

Manolin is present only in the beginning and at the end of *The Old Man and the Sea,* but his presence is important because Manolin's devotion to Santiago highlights Santiago's value as a person and as a fisherman. Manolin demonstrates his love for Santiago openly. He makes sure that the old man has food, blankets, and can rest without being bothered. Despite Hemingway's insistence that his characters were a real old man and a real boy, Manolin's purity and singleness of purpose elevate him to the level of a symbolic character. Manolin's actions are not tainted by the confusion, ambivalence, or willfulness that typify adolescence. Instead, he is a companion who feels nothing but love and devotion.

Hemingway does hint at the boy's resentment for his father, whose wishes Manolin obeys by abandoning the old man after forty days without catching a fish. This fact helps to establish the boy as a real human being—a person with conflicted loyalties who faces difficult decisions. By the end of the book, however, the boy abandons his duty to his father, swearing that he will sail with the old man regardless of the consequences. He stands, in the novella's final pages, as a symbol of uncompromised love and fidelity. As the old man's apprentice, he also represents the life that will follow from death. His dedication to learning from the old man ensures that Santiago will live on.

Themes, Motifs & Symbols

Themes

Themes are the fundamental and often universal ideas explored in a literary work.

The Honor in Struggle, Defeat & Death

From the very first paragraph, Santiago is characterized as someone struggling against defeat. He has gone eighty-four days without catching a fish—he will soon pass his own record of eighty-seven days. Almost as a reminder of Santiago's struggle, the sail of his skiff resembles "the flag of permanent defeat." But the old man refuses defeat at every turn: he resolves to sail out beyond the other fishermen to where the biggest fish promise to be. He lands the marlin, tying his record of eighty-seven days after a brutal three-day fight, and he continues to ward off sharks from stealing his prey, even though he knows the battle is useless.

Because Santiago is pitted against the creatures of the sea, some readers choose to view the tale as a chronicle of man's battle *against* the natural world, but the novella is, more accurately, the story of man's place *within* nature. Both Santiago and the marlin display qualities of pride, honor, and bravery, and both are subject to the same eternal law: they must kill or be killed. As Santiago reflects when he watches the weary warbler fly toward shore, where it will inevitably meet the hawk, the world is filled with predators, and no living thing can escape the inevitable struggle that will lead to its death. Santiago lives according to his own observation: "man is not made for defeat . . . [a] man can be destroyed but not defeated." In Hemingway's portrait of the world, death is inevitable, but the best men (and animals) will nonetheless refuse to give in to its power. Accordingly, man and fish will struggle to the death, just as hungry sharks will lay waste to an old man's trophy catch.

The novel suggests that it is possible to transcend this natural law. In fact, the very inevitability of destruction creates the terms that allow a worthy man or beast to transcend it. It is precisely through the effort to battle the inevitable that a man can prove himself.

9

Indeed, a man can prove this determination over and over through the worthiness of the opponents he chooses to face. Santiago finds the marlin worthy of a fight, just as he once found "the great negro of Cienfuegos" worthy. His admiration for these opponents brings love and respect into an equation with death, as their destruction becomes a point of honor and bravery that confirms Santiago's heroic qualities. One might characterize the equation as the working out of the statement "Because I love you, I have to kill you." Alternately, one might draw a parallel to the poet John Keats and his insistence that beauty can only be comprehended in the moment before death, as beauty bows to destruction. Santiago, though destroyed at the end of the novella, is never defeated. Instead, he emerges as a hero. Santiago's struggle does not enable him to change man's place in the world. Rather, it enables him to meet his most dignified destiny.

Pride as the Source of Greatness & Determination

Many parallels exist between Santiago and the classic heroes of the ancient world. In addition to exhibiting terrific strength, bravery, and moral certainty, those heroes usually possess a tragic flaw—a quality that, though admirable, leads to their eventual downfall. If pride is Santiago's fatal flaw, he is keenly aware of it. After sharks have destroyed the marlin, the old man apologizes again and again to his worthy opponent. He has ruined them both, he concedes, by sailing beyond the usual boundaries of fishermen. Indeed, his last word on the subject comes when he asks himself the reason for his undoing and decides, "Nothing . . . I went out too far."

While it is certainly true that Santiago's eighty-four-day run of bad luck is an affront to his pride as a masterful fisherman, and that his attempt to bear out his skills by sailing far into the gulf waters leads to disaster, Hemingway does not condemn his protagonist for being full of pride. On the contrary, Santiago stands as proof that pride motivates men to greatness. Because the old man acknowledges that he killed the mighty marlin largely out of pride, and because his capture of the marlin leads in turn to his heroic transcendence of defeat, pride becomes the source of Santiago's greatest strength. Without a ferocious sense of pride, that battle would never have been fought, or more likely, it would have been abandoned before the end.

Santiago's pride also motivates his desire to transcend the destructive forces of nature. Throughout the novel, no matter how baleful his circumstances become, the old man exhibits an unflagging determination to catch the marlin and bring it to shore. When the first shark arrives, Santiago's resolve is mentioned twice in the space of just a few paragraphs. First we are told that the old man "was full of resolution but he had little hope." Then, sentences later, the narrator says, "He hit [the shark] without hope but with resolution." The old man meets every challenge with the same unwavering determination: he is willing to die in order to bring in the marlin, and he is willing to die in order to battle the feeding sharks. It is this conscious decision to act, to fight, to never give up that enables Santiago to avoid defeat. Although he returns to Havana without the trophy of his long battle, he returns with the knowledge that he has acquitted himself proudly and manfully. Hemingway seems to suggest that victory is not a prerequisite for honor. Instead, glory depends upon one having the pride to see a struggle through to its end, regardless of the outcome. Even if the old man had returned with the marlin intact, his moment of glory, like the marlin's meat, would have been short-lived. The glory and honor Santiago accrues comes not from his battle itself but from his pride and determination to fight.

MOTIFS

Motifs are recurring structures, contrasts, and literary devices that can help to develop and inform the text's major themes.

CRUCIFIXION IMAGERY

In order to suggest the profundity of the old man's sacrifice and the glory that derives from it, Hemingway purposefully likens Santiago to Christ, who, according to Christian theology, gave his life for the greater glory of humankind. Crucifixion imagery is the most noticeable way in which Hemingway creates the symbolic parallel between Santiago and Christ. When Santiago's palms are first cut by his fishing line, the reader cannot help but think of Christ suffering his stigmata. Later, when the sharks arrive, Hemingway portrays the old man as a crucified martyr, saying that he makes a noise similar to that of a man having nails driven through his hands. Furthermore, the image of the old man struggling up the hill with his mast across his shoulders recalls Christ's march toward Calvary. Even the position in which Santiago collapses on his bed—face down with his arms out straight and the palms of his hands up—brings to mind the image of Christ suffering on the cross. Hemingway employs these images in the final pages of the novella in order to link Santiago to

Christ, who exemplified transcendence by turning loss into gain, defeat into triumph, and even death into renewed life.

LIFE FROM DEATH
Death is the unavoidable force in the novella, the one fact that no living creature can escape. But death, Hemingway suggests, is never an end in itself: in death there is always the possibility of the most vigorous life. The reader notes that as Santiago slays the marlin, not only is the old man reinvigorated by the battle, but the fish also comes alive "with his death in him." Life, the possibility of renewal, necessarily follows on the heels of death.

Whereas the marlin's death hints at a type of physical reanimation, death leads to life in less literal ways at other points in the novella. The book's crucifixion imagery emphasizes the cyclical connection between life and death, as does Santiago's battle with the marlin. His success at bringing the marlin in earns him the awed respect of the fishermen who once mocked him, and secures him the companionship of Manolin, the apprentice who will carry on Santiago's teachings long after the old man has died.

THE LIONS ON THE BEACH
Santiago dreams his pleasant dream of the lions at play on the beaches of Africa three times. The first time is the night before he departs on his three-day fishing expedition, the second occurs when he sleeps on the boat for a few hours in the middle of his struggle with the marlin, and the third takes place at the very end of the book. In fact, the sober promise of the triumph and regeneration with which the novella closes is supported by the final image of the lions. Because Santiago associates the lions with his youth, the dream suggests the circular nature of life. Additionally, because Santiago imagines the lions, fierce predators, playing, his dream suggests a harmony between the opposing forces—life and death, love and hate, destruction and regeneration—of nature.

MOTIFS

SYMBOLS

Symbols are objects, characters, figures, and colors used to represent abstract ideas and concepts.

THE MARLIN

Magnificent and glorious, the marlin symbolizes the ideal opponent. In a world in which "everything kills everything else in some way," Santiago feels genuinely lucky to find himself matched against a creature that brings out the best in him: his strength, courage, love, and respect.

THE SHOVEL-NOSED SHARKS

The shovel-nosed sharks are little more than moving appetites that thoughtlessly and gracelessly attack the marlin. As opponents of the old man, they stand in bold contrast to the marlin, which is worthy of Santiago's effort and strength. They symbolize and embody the destructive laws of the universe and attest to the fact that those laws can be transcended only when equals fight to the death. Because they are base predators, Santiago wins no glory from battling them.

SUMMARY & ANALYSIS

The Old Man and the Sea is a narrative without pauses, chapter breaks, or other marked divisions. For ease of discussion, this SparkNote divides the text into five sections that correspond to the five days that the narrative spans.

DAY ONE

From Santiago's return from the eighty-fourth consecutive day without catching a fish to his dreams of lions on the beach

SUMMARY

> *He only dreamed of places now and of the lions on the beach. They played like young cats in the dusk and he loved them as he loved the boy.*
>
> *(See QUOTATIONS, p. 33)*

Santiago, an old fisherman, has gone eighty-four days without catching a fish. For the first forty days, a boy named Manolin had fished with him, but Manolin's parents, who call Santiago *salao,* or "the worst form of unlucky," forced Manolin to leave him in order to work in a more prosperous boat. The old man is wrinkled, splotched, and scarred from handling heavy fish on cords, but his eyes, which are the color of the sea, remain "cheerful and undefeated."

Having made some money with the successful fishermen, the boy offers to return to Santiago's skiff, reminding him of their previous eighty-seven-day run of bad luck, which culminated in their catching big fish every day for three weeks. He talks with the old man as they haul in Santiago's fishing gear and laments that he was forced to obey his father, who lacks faith and, as a result, made him switch boats. The pair stops for a beer at a terrace café, where fishermen make fun of Santiago. The old man does not mind. Santiago and Manolin reminisce about the many years the two of them fished together, and the boy begs the old man to let him provide fresh bait fish for him. The old man accepts the gift with humility. Santiago announces his plans to go "far out" in the sea the following day.

Manolin and Santiago haul the gear to the old man's shack, which is furnished with nothing more than the barest necessities: a bed, a table and chair, and a place to cook. On the wall are two pictures: one of the Sacred Heart of Jesus and one of the Virgin of Cobre, the patroness of Cuba. The old man has taken down the photograph of his wife, which made him feel "too lonely." The two go through their usual dinner ritual, in which the boy asks Santiago what he is going to eat, and the old man replies, "yellow rice with fish," and then offers some to the boy. The boy declines, and his offer to start the old man's fire is rejected. In reality, there is no food.

Excited to read the baseball scores, Santiago pulls out a newspaper, which he says was given to him by Perico at the bodega. Manolin goes to get the bait fish and returns with some dinner as well, a gift from Martin, the café owner. The old man is moved by Martin's thoughtfulness and promises to repay the kindness. Manolin and Santiago discuss baseball. Santiago is a huge admirer of "the great DiMaggio," whose father was a fisherman. After discussing with Santiago the greatest ballplayers and the greatest baseball managers, the boy declares that Santiago is the greatest fisherman: "There are many good fishermen and some great ones. But there is only you." Finally, the boy leaves, and the old man goes to sleep. He dreams his sweet, recurring dream, of lions playing on the white beaches of Africa, a scene he saw from his ship when he was a very young man.

ANALYSIS

The opening pages of the book establish Santiago's character and set the scene for the action to follow. Even though he loves Manolin and is loved dearly by the boy, the old man lives as an outsider. The greeting he receives from the fishermen, most of whom mock him for his fruitless voyages to sea, shows Santiago to be an alienated, almost ostracized figure. Such an alienated position is characteristic of Hemingway's heroes, whose greatest achievements depend, in large part, upon their isolation. In Hemingway's works, it is only once a man is removed from the numbing and false confines of modern society that he can confront the larger, universal truths that govern him. In *A Farewell to Arms,* for instance, only after Frederic Henry abandons his post in the army and lives in seclusion is he able to learn the dismal lesson that death renders meaningless such notions as honor, glory, and love. Yet, although Hemingway's message in *The Old Man and the Sea* is tragic in many respects, the story of

THE OLD MAN AND THE SEA

Santiago and the destruction of his greatest catch is far from dismal. Unlike Frederic, Santiago is not defeated by his enlightenment. The narrator emphasizes Santiago's perseverance in the opening pages, mentioning that the old man's eyes are still "cheerful and undefeated" after suffering nearly three months without a single catch. And, although Santiago's struggle will bring about defeat—the great marlin will be devoured by sharks—Santiago will emerge as a victor. As he tells the boy, in order for this to happen, he must venture far out, farther than the other fishermen are willing to go.

In Hemingway's narrative, Santiago is elevated above the normal stature of a protagonist, assuming near-mythical proportions. He belongs to a tradition of literary heroes whose superior qualities necessitate their distance from ordinary humans and endeavors. Because Manolin constantly expresses his devotion to, reverence for, and trust of Santiago, he establishes his mentor as a figure of significant moral and professional stature, despite the difficulties of the past eighty-four days. While other young fishermen make fun of the old man, Manolin knows Santiago's true worth and the extent of Santiago's knowledge. In the old man, Hemingway provides the reader with a model of good, simple living: Santiago transcends the evils of the world—hunger, poverty, the contempt of his fellow men—by enduring them.

In these first few scenes, Hemingway introduces several issues and images that will recur throughout the book. The first is the question of Santiago's endurance. The descriptions of his crude hut, almost nonexistent eating habits, and emaciated body force the reader to question the old man's physical capacities. How could Santiago, who subsists on occasional handouts from kind café owners or, worse, imaginary meals, wage the terrific battle with the great marlin that the novel recounts? As the book progresses, we see that the question is irrelevant. Although Santiago's battle is played out in physical terms, the stakes are decidedly spiritual.

This section also introduces two important symbols: the lions playing on the beaches of Africa and baseball's immortal Joe DiMaggio. Throughout his trial at sea, Santiago's thoughts will return to DiMaggio, for to him the baseball player represents a kind of triumphant survival. After suffering a bone spur in his heel, DiMaggio returned to baseball to become, in the eyes of many, the greatest player of all time. The lions are a more enigmatic symbol. The narrator says that they are Santiago's only remaining dream. When he sleeps, he no longer envisions storms or women or fish, but only the "young cats in the dusk," which "he love[s] . . . as he love[s] the boy." Because the image of the lions has stayed with Santiago since his boyhood, the lions connect the end of the old man's life with the beginning, giving his existence a kind of circularity. Like Santiago, the lions are hunters at the core of their being. The fact that Santiago dreams of the lions at play rather than on the hunt indicates that his dream is a break—albeit a temporary one—from the vicious order of the natural world.

DAY TWO

From Santiago waking Manolin at the start of the eighty-fifth day since Santiago has caught a fish to Santiago's promise to kill the marlin before the day ends

SUMMARY

The old man hit him on the head for kindness and kicked him, his body still shuddering, under the shade of the stern.

(See QUOTATIONS, p. 34)

The next morning, before sunrise, the old man goes to Manolin's house to wake the boy. The two head back to Santiago's shack, carry the old man's gear to his boat, and drink coffee from condensed milk cans. Santiago has slept well and is confident about the day's prospects. He and Manolin part on the beach, wishing each other good luck.

The old man rows steadily away from shore, toward the deep waters of the Gulf Stream. He hears the leaps and whirs of the flying fish, which he considers to be his friends, and thinks with sympathy of the small, frail birds that try to catch them. He loves the sea, though at times it can be cruel. He thinks of the sea as a woman whose wild behavior is beyond her control. The old man drops his baited fishing lines to various measured depths and rows expertly to keep them from drifting with the current. Above all else, he is precise.

The sun comes up. Santiago continues to move away from shore, observing his world as he drifts along. He sees flying fish pursued by dolphins; a diving, circling seabird; Sargasso weed, a type of seaweed found in the Gulf Stream; the distasteful purple Portuguese man-of-war; and the small fish that swim among the jellyfish-like creatures' filaments. Rowing farther and farther out, Santiago follows the seabird that is hunting for fish, using it as a guide. Soon, one of the old man's lines goes taut. He pulls up a ten-pound tuna, which, he says out loud, will make a lovely piece of bait. He wonders when he developed the habit of talking to himself but does not remember. He thinks that if the other fishermen heard him talking, they would think him crazy, although he knows he isn't. Eventually, the old man realizes that he has sailed so far out that he can no longer see the green of the shore.

When the projecting stick that marks the top of the hundred-fathom line dips sharply, Santiago is sure that the fish tugging on the line is of a considerable size, and he prays that it will take the bait. The marlin plays with the bait for a while, and when it does finally take the bait, it starts to move with it, pulling the boat. The old man gives a mighty pull, then another, but he gains nothing. The fish drags the skiff farther into the sea. No land at all is visible to Santiago now.

All day the fish pulls the boat as the old man braces the line with his back and holds it taut in his hands, ready to give more line if necessary. The struggle goes on all night, as the fish continues to pull the boat. The glow given off by the lights of Havana gradually fades, signifying that the boat is the farthest from shore it has been so far. Over and over, the old man wishes he had the boy with him. When he sees two porpoises playing in the water, Santiago begins to pity his quarry and consider it a brother. He thinks back to the time that he caught one of a pair of marlin: the male fish let the female take the bait, then he stayed by the boat, as though in mourning. Although the memory makes him sad, Santiago's determination is unchecked: as the marlin swims out, the old man goes "beyond all people in the world" to find him.

The sun rises and the fish has not tired, though it is now swimming in shallower waters. The old man cannot increase the tension on the line, because if it is too taut it will break and the fish will get away. Also, if the hook makes too big a cut in the fish, the fish may get away from it. Santiago hopes that the fish will jump, because its air sacs would fill and prevent the fish from going too deep into the water, which would make it easier to pull out. A yellow weed attaches to the line, helping to slow the fish. Santiago can do nothing but hold on. He pledges his love and respect to the fish, but he nevertheless promises that he will kill his opponent before the day ends.

ANALYSIS

As Santiago sets out on the eighty-fifth day, the reader witnesses the qualities that earn him Manolin's praise and dedication. The old man is an expert seaman, able to read the sea, sky, and their respective creatures like books that tell him what he needs to know. The flying fish, for instance, signal the arrival of dolphins, while, in Santiago's experience, the magnificent tug on the line can mean only one thing: a marlin—a type of large game fish that weighs hundreds of pounds. Unlike the fishermen he passes on his way into the deep waters of the gulf, Santiago exercises an unparalleled precision when fishing. He keeps his lines perfectly straight instead of letting them drift as the other fishermen do, which means that he always knows exactly how deep they are. Santiago's focus, his strength and resolve in the face of tremendous obstacles, as well as the sheer artistry with which he executes his tasks, mark him as a hero.

Santiago conforms to the model of the classical hero in two important respects. First, he displays a rare determination to understand the universe, as is evident when he meditates that the sea is beautiful and benevolent, but also so cruel that the birds who rely on the sea's bounty are too delicate for it. Second, the old man possesses a tragic flaw that will lead to his downfall: pride. Santiago's pride carries him far, not only metaphorically but literally—beyond his fellow fishermen into beautiful but, in the end, terribly cruel waters. As in classical epics, the most important struggle in Hemingway's novella is a moral one. The fish itself is of secondary importance, for it is merely a trophy, a material prize.

Some critics have taken issue with Hemingway's depiction of the old man because it betrays the very tenets of fiction that the author demanded (see "Hemingway's Style"). Hemingway was, first and foremost, a proponent of realism. He wished to strip literature of its pretense and ornamentation, and he built a reputation as a journalistic writer who prized hard facts above all else. Metaphysical meditations and lofty philosophizing held little interest for Hemingway when compared to the details of daily life. As he states in *A Farewell to Arms*, "Abstract words such as glory, honor, courage or hallow were obscene beside the concrete names of villages, the number of roads, the names of rivers, the numbers of regiments and the dates." But several critics have charged Hemingway with a failure to render his old man or, for that matter, the sea realistically. Hemingway has forged particular details that simply are not true. For example, as critic Robert P. Weeks points out, the poisonous Portuguese man-of-war that follows Santiago's boat would not appear in the waters off of Cuba for another six months. A more significant, less petty objection is the charge that Hemingway reduces Santiago to an unrealistic archetype of goodness and purity, while the surrounding world is marked by man's romance and brotherhood with the sea and its many creatures.

Many critics believe that Hemingway was striking out into new literary territory with *The Old Man and the Sea*. America's foremost proponent of realism seemed to be moving toward something as highly symbolic as parable. Hemingway, however, disagreed. The philosophy that governed his writing of the novella was the same one that shaped his earlier novels. In a 1958 interview with *The Paris Review*, Hemingway spoke about *The Old Man and the Sea*:

> Anyway, to skip how [the writing] is done, I had unbelievable luck this time and could convey the [old man's] experience completely and have it be one that no one had ever conveyed. The luck was that I had a good man and a good boy and lately writers have forgotten there are still such things.

To Hemingway, Santiago and Manolin were as true to the real world as protagonists like Frederic Henry of *A Farewell to Arms* or Jake Barnes of *The Sun Also Rises*.

The old man's memory of hooking the female marlin of a male-female pair exemplifies Hemingway's vision of a world in which women have no real place—even the picture of Santiago's wife no longer remains on his wall. Men are the central focus of most of Hemingway's writing and certainly of *The Old Man and the Sea*. It is no coincidence that Santiago is convinced that his greatest adversary is, as he continually notes, a male, a fact that he could not possibly ascertain before even seeing the fish.

Day Three

From Santiago's encounter with the weary warbler to his
decision to rest after contemplating the night sky

Summary

> I do not understand these things, he thought. But it is
> good that we do not have to try to kill the sun or the
> moon or the stars. It is enough to live on the sea and
> kill our true brothers.
>
> (See QUOTATIONS, p. 35)

A small, tired warbler (a type of bird) lands on the stern of the skiff, flutters around Santiago's head, then perches on the taut fishing line that links the old man to the big fish. The old man suspects that it is the warbler's first trip, and that it knows nothing of the hawks that will meet the warbler as it nears land. Knowing that the warbler cannot understand him, the old man tells the bird to stay and rest up before heading toward shore. Just then the marlin surges, nearly pulling Santiago overboard, and the bird departs. Santiago notices that his hand is bleeding from where the line has cut it.

Aware that he will need to keep his strength, the old man makes himself eat the tuna he caught the day before, which he had expected to use as bait. While he cuts and eats the fish with his right hand, his already cut left hand cramps and tightens into a claw under the strain of taking all the fish's resistance. Santiago is angered and frustrated by the weakness of his own body, but the tuna, he hopes, will reinvigorate the hand. As he eats, he feels a brotherly desire to feed the marlin too.

While waiting for the cramp in his hand to ease, Santiago looks across the vast waters and thinks himself to be completely alone. A flight of ducks passes overhead, and he realizes that it is impossible for a man to be alone on the sea. The slant of the fishing line changes, indicating to the old fisherman that the fish is approaching the surface. Suddenly, the fish leaps magnificently into the air, and Santiago sees that it is bigger than any he has ever witnessed; it is two feet longer than the skiff itself. Santiago declares it "great" and promises never to let the fish learn its own strength. The line races out until the fish slows to its earlier pace. By noon, the old man's hand is uncramped, and though he claims he is not religious, he says ten Hail Marys and ten Our Fathers and promises that, if he catches the fish, he will make a pilgrimage to the Virgin of Cobre. In case his struggle with the marlin should continue for another night, Santiago baits another line in hopes of catching another meal.

The second day of Santiago's struggle with the marlin wears on. The old man alternately questions and justifies seeking the death of such a noble opponent. As dusk approaches, Santiago's thoughts turn to baseball. The great DiMaggio, thinks the old man, plays brilliantly despite the pain of a bone spur in his heel. Santiago is not actually sure what a bone spur is, but he is sure he would not be able to bear the pain of one himself. (A bone spur is an outgrowth that projects from the bone.) He wonders if DiMaggio would stay with the marlin. To boost his confidence, the old man recalls the great all-night arm-wrestling match he won as a young man. Having beaten "the great negro from Cienfuegos [a town in Cuba]," Santiago earned the title *El Campeón*, or "The Champion."

Just before nightfall, a dolphin takes the second bait Santiago had dropped. The old man hauls it in with one hand and clubs it dead. He saves the meat for the following day. Although Santiago boasts to the marlin that he feels prepared for their impending fight, he is really numb with pain. The stars come out. Santiago considers the stars his friends, as he does the great marlin. He considers himself lucky that his lot in life does not involve hunting anything so great as the stars or the moon. Again, he feels sorry for the marlin, though he is as determined as ever to kill it. The fish will feed many people, Santiago decides, though they are not worthy of the creature's great dignity. By starlight, still bracing and handling the line, Santiago considers rigging the oars so that the fish will have to pull harder and eventually tire itself out. He fears this strategy would ultimately result in the loss of the fish. He decides to "rest," which really just means putting down his hands and letting the line go across his back, instead of using his own strength to resist his opponent.

After "resting" for two hours, Santiago chastises himself for not sleeping, and he fears what could happen should his mind become "unclear." He butchers the dolphin he caught earlier and finds two flying fish in its belly. In the chilling night, he eats half of a fillet of dolphin meat and one of the flying fish. While the marlin is quiet, the old man decides to sleep. He has several dreams: a school of porpoises leaps from and returns to the ocean; he is back in his hut during a storm; and he again dreams of the lions on the beach in Africa.

ANALYSIS

The narrator tells us that Santiago does not mention the hawks that await the little warbler because he thinks the bird will learn about them "soon enough." Hemingway tempers the grimness of Santiago's observation with Santiago's feeling of deep connection with the warbler. He suggests that the world, though designed to bring about death, is a vast, interconnected network of life. Additionally, the warbler's feeling of exhaustion and its ultimate fate—destruction by predators—mirror Santiago's own eventual exhaustion and the marlin's ravishment by sharks.

The brotherhood between Santiago and the surrounding world extends beyond the warbler. The old man feels an intimate connection to the great fish, as well as to the sea and stars. Santiago constantly pledges his love, respect, and sentiment of brotherhood to the marlin. For this reason, the fish's death is not portrayed as senselessly tragic. Santiago, and seemingly Hemingway, feel that since death *must* come in the world, it is preferable that it come at the hands of a worthy opponent. The old man's magnificence—the honor and humility with which he executes his task—elevates his struggle to a rarified, even transcendent level.

Skills that involved great displays of strength captured Hemingway's imagination, and his fiction is filled with fishermen, big-game hunters, bullfighters, prizefighters, and soldiers. Hemingway's fiction presents a world peopled almost exclusively by men—men who live most successfully in the world through displays of skill. In Hemingway's world, mere survival is not enough. To elevate oneself above the masses, one must master the rules and rituals by which men are judged. Time and again, we see Santiago displaying the art and the rituals that make him a master of his trade. Only *his* lines do not drift carelessly in the current; only *he* braves waters so far from shore.

Rules and rituals dominate the rest of the old man's life as well. When he is not thinking about fishing, his mind turns to religion or baseball. Because Santiago declares that he is not a religious man, his prayers to the Virgin of Cobre seem less an appeal to a supernatural divinity and more a habit that orders and provides a context for his daily experience. Similarly, Santiago's worship of Joe DiMaggio, and his constant comparisons between the baseball great and himself, suggest his preference for worlds in which men are measured by a clear set of standards. The great DiMaggio's reputation is secured by his superlative batting average as surely as Santiago's will be by an eighteen-foot marlin.

Even though Santiago doesn't consider himself a religious man, it is during his struggle with the marlin that the book becomes strongly suggestive of a Christian parable. As his struggle intensifies, Santiago begins to seem more and more Christ-like: through his pain, suffering, and eventual defeat, he will transcend his previous incarnation as a failed fisherman. Hemingway achieves this effect by relying on the potent and, to many readers, familiar symbolism identified with Jesus Christ's life and death. The cuts on the old man's hands from the fishing line recall the stigmata—the crucifixion wounds of Jesus. Santiago's isolation, too, evokes that of Christ, who spent forty days alone in the wilderness. Having taken his boat out on the ocean farther than any other fisherman has ever gone, Santiago is beyond even the fringes of society.

Hemingway also unites the old man with marlin through Santiago's frequent expressions of his feeling of kinship. He thus suggests that the fate of one is the fate of the other. Although they are opponents, Santiago and the marlin are also partners, allies, and, in a sense, doubles. Thus, the following passage, which links the marlin to Christ, implicitly links Santiago to Christ as well:

> "Christ, I did not know he was so big."
> "I'll kill him though," [Santiago] said. "In all his greatness and his glory."

Santiago's expletive ("Christ") and the laudatory phrase "his greatness and his glory" link the fish's fate to Christ's. Because Santiago declares the marlin his "true brother," he implies that they share a common fate. When, later in the book, sharks attack the marlin's carcass, thereby attacking Santiago as well, the sense of alliance between the old man and the fish becomes even more explicit.

SUMMARY & ANALYSIS

Day Four

*From the marlin waking Santiago by jerking the line to
Santiago's return to his shack*

Summary

> Then the fish came alive, with his death in him, and
> rose high out of the water showing all his great length
> and width and all his power and his beauty.
>
> (See QUOTATIONS, p. 36)

The marlin wakes Santiago by jerking the line. The fish jumps out of
the water again and again, and Santiago is thrown into the bow of
the skiff, facedown in his dolphin meat. The line feeds out fast, and
the old man brakes against it with his back and hands. His left hand,
especially, is badly cut. Santiago wishes that the boy were with him
to wet the coils of the line, which would lessen the friction.

The old man wipes the crushed dolphin meat off his face, fearing
that it will make him nauseated and he will lose his strength. Looking at his damaged hand, he reflects that "pain does not matter to
a man." He eats the second flying fish in hopes of building up his
strength. As the sun rises, the marlin begins to circle. For hours the
old man fights the circling fish for every inch of line, slowly pulling it
in. He feels faint and dizzy and sees black spots before his eyes. The
fish riots against the line, battering the boat with its spear. When it
passes under the boat, Santiago cannot believe its size. As the marlin continues to circle, Santiago adds enough pressure to the line to
bring the fish closer and closer to the skiff. The old man thinks that
the fish is killing him, and admires him for it, saying, "I do not care
who kills who." Eventually, he pulls the fish onto its side by the boat
and plunges his harpoon into it. The fish lurches out of the water,
brilliantly and beautifully alive as it dies. When it falls back into the
water, its blood stains the waves.

The old man pulls the skiff up alongside the fish and fastens the
fish to the side of the boat. He thinks about how much money he will
be able to make from such a big fish, and he imagines that DiMaggio would be proud of him. Santiago's hands are so cut up that they
resemble raw meat. With the mast up and the sail drawn, man, fish,
and boat head for land. In his light-headed state, the old man finds
himself wondering for a moment if he is bringing the fish in or vice
versa. He shakes some shrimp from a patch of gulf weed and eats

them raw. He watches the marlin carefully as the ship sails on. The old man's wounds remind him that his battle with the marlin was real and not a dream.

An hour later, a mako shark arrives, having smelled the marlin's blood. Except for its jaws full of talonlike teeth, the shark is a beautiful fish. When the shark hits the marlin, the old man sinks his harpoon into the shark's head. The shark lashes on the water and, eventually, sinks, taking the harpoon and the old man's rope with it. The mako has taken nearly forty pounds of meat, so fresh blood from the marlin spills into the water, inevitably drawing more sharks to attack. Santiago realizes that his struggle with the marlin was for nothing; all will soon be lost. But, he muses, "a man can be destroyed but not defeated."

Santiago tries to cheer himself by thinking that DiMaggio would be pleased by his performance, and he wonders again if his hands equal DiMaggio's bone spurs as a handicap. He tries to be hopeful, thinking that it is silly, if not sinful, to stop hoping. He reminds himself that he didn't kill the marlin simply for food, that he killed it out of pride and love. He wonders if it is a sin to kill something you love. The shark, on the other hand, he does not feel guilty about killing, because he did it in self-defense. He decides that "everything kills everything else in some way."

Two hours later, a pair of shovel-nosed sharks arrives, and Santiago makes a noise likened to the sound a man might make as nails are driven through his hands. The sharks attack, and Santiago fights them with a knife that he had lashed to an oar as a makeshift weapon. He enjoyed killing the mako because it was a worthy opponent, a mighty and fearless predator, but he has nothing but disdain for the scavenging shovel-nosed sharks. The old man kills them both, but not before they take a good quarter of the marlin, including the best meat. Again, Santiago wishes that he hadn't killed the marlin. He apologizes to the dead marlin for having gone out so far, saying it did neither of them any good.

Still hopeful that the whole ordeal had been a dream, Santiago cannot bear to look at the mutilated marlin. Another shovel-nosed shark arrives. The old man kills it, but he loses his knife in the process. Just before nightfall, two more sharks approach. The old man's arsenal has been reduced to the club he uses to kill bait fish. He manages to club the sharks into retreat, but not before they repeatedly maul the marlin. Stiff, sore, and weary, he hopes he does not have to fight anymore. He even dares to imagine making it home with the half-fish that remains. Again, he apologizes to the marlin carcass and attempts to console it by reminding the fish how many sharks he has killed. He wonders how many sharks the marlin killed when it was alive, and he pledges to fight the sharks until he dies. Although he hopes to be lucky, Santiago believes that he "violated [his] luck" when he sailed too far out.

Around midnight, a pack of sharks arrives. Near-blind in the darkness, Santiago strikes out at the sounds of jaws and fins. Something snatches his club. He breaks off the boat's tiller and makes a futile attempt to use it as a weapon. When the last shark tries to tear at the tough head of the marlin, the old man clubs the shark until the tiller splinters. He plunges the sharp edge into the shark's flesh and the beast lets go. No meat is left on the marlin.

The old man spits blood into the water, which frightens him for a moment. He settles in to steer the boat, numb and past all feeling. He asks himself what it was that defeated him and concludes, "Nothing . . . I went out too far." When he reaches the harbor, all lights are out and no one is near. He notices the skeleton of the fish still tied to the skiff. He takes down the mast and begins to shoulder it up the hill to his shack. It is terrifically heavy, and he is forced to sit down five times before he reaches his home. Once there, the old man sleeps.

ANALYSIS

You loved him when he was alive and you loved him after. If you love him, it is not a sin to kill him. Or is it more?

(See QUOTATIONS, p. 37)

The fantastical final stage of the old man's fight with the fish brings two thematic issues to the forefront. The first concerns man's place in nature, the second concerns nature itself. It is possible to interpret Santiago's journey as a cautionary tale of sorts, a tragic lesson about what happens when man's pride forces him beyond the boundaries of his rightful, human place in the world. This interpretation is undermined, however, by the fact that Santiago finds the place where he is most completely, honestly, and fully himself only by sailing out farther than he ever has before. Indeed, Santiago has not left his true place; he has *found* it, which suggests that man's greatest potential can be found in his return to the natural world from which modern advancements have driven him.

At one point, Santiago embraces his unity with the marlin, thinking, "You are killing me, fish . . . But you have a right to . . . brother. Come on and kill me. I do not care who kills who." This realization speaks to the novella's theory of the natural world. As Santiago's exhausting and near-endless battle with the marlin shows, his is a world in which life and death go hand in loving hand. Everything in the world must die, and according to Santiago, only a brotherhood between men—or creatures—can alleviate the grimness of that fact. The death of the marlin serves as a beautiful case in point, for as the fish dies it is not only transformed into something larger than itself, it is also charged with life: "Then the fish came alive, with his death in him." In Hemingway's conception of the natural world, beauty is deadly, age is strength, and death is the greatest instance of vitality.

The transformation that the fish undergoes upon its death anticipates the transformation that awaits Santiago in the novella's final pages. The old man's battle with the fish is marked by supreme pain and suffering, but he lives in a world in which extreme pain can be a source of triumph rather than defeat. The key to Santiago's triumph, as the end of the novel makes clear, is an almost martyrlike endurance, a quality that the old man knows and values. Santiago repeatedly reminds himself that physical pain does not matter to a man, and he urges himself to keep his head clear and to know how to suffer like a man.

After the arrival of the mako shark, Santiago seems preoccupied with the notion of hope. Hope is shown to be a necessary component of endurance, so much so that the novella seems to suggest that endurance can be found wherever pain and hope meet. As Santiago sails on while the sharks continue to attack his catch, the narrator says that Santiago "was full of resolution but he had little hope"; later, the narrator comments, "He hit [the shark] without hope but with resolution." But without hope Santiago has reason neither to fight the sharks nor to return home. He soon realizes that it is silly not to hope, and he even goes so far as to consider it a sin. Ultimately, he overcomes the shark attack by *bearing* it. The poet and critic Delmore Schwartz regards *The Old Man and the Sea* as a dramatic development in Hemingway's career because Santiago's "sober hope" strikes a sort of compromise between youthful naïveté and the jadedness of age. Before the novella, Hemingway had given the world heroes who lived either shrouded by illusions, such as Nick Adams in "Indian Camp," or crushed by disillusionment, such as Frederic Henry in *A Farewell to Arms*.

DAY FIVE

*From Manolin bringing the old man coffee to the old man's
return to sleep to dream, once again, about the lions*

SUMMARY

Early the next morning, Manolin comes to the old man's shack, and
the sight of his friend's ravaged hands brings him to tears. He goes
to fetch coffee. Fishermen have gathered around Santiago's boat
and measured the carcass at eighteen feet. Manolin waits for the
old man to wake up, keeping his coffee warm for him so it is ready
right away. When the old man wakes, he and Manolin talk warmly.
Santiago says that the sharks beat him, and Manolin insists that he
will work with the old man again, regardless of what his parents
say. He reveals that there had been a search for Santiago involving
the coast guard and planes. Santiago is happy to have someone to
talk to, and after he and Manolin make plans, the old man sleeps
again. Manolin leaves to find food and the newspapers for the old
man, and to tell Pedrico that the marlin's head is his. That afternoon
two tourists at the terrace café mistake the great skeleton for that of
a shark. Manolin continues to watch over the old man as he sleeps
and dreams of the lions.

ANALYSIS

Given the depth of Santiago's tragedy—most likely Santiago will
never have the opportunity to catch another such fish in his lifetime—*The Old Man and the Sea* ends on a rather optimistic note.
Santiago is reunited with Manolin, who desperately wants to complete his training. All of the old man's noble qualities and, more
important, the lessons he draws from his experience, will be passed
on to the boy, which means that the fisherman's life will continue
on, in some form, even after his death. The promise of triumph and
regeneration is supported by the closing image of the book. For the
third time, Santiago returns to his dream of the lions at play on the
African beaches. As an image that recalls the old man's youth, the
lions suggest the circularity of life. They also suggest the harmony—
the lions are, after all, playing—that exists between the opposing
forces of nature.

The hope that Santiago clings to at the novella's close is not the
hope that comes from naïveté. It is, rather, a hope that comes from
experience, of something new emerging from something old, as a

phoenix rises out of the ashes. The novella states as much when Santiago reflects that "a man can be destroyed but not defeated." The destruction of the marlin is not a defeat for Santiago; rather, it leads to his redemption. Indeed, the fishermen who once mocked him now stand in awe of him. The decimation of the marlin, of course, is a significant loss. The sharks strip Santiago of his greater glory as surely as they strip the great fish of its flesh. But to view the shark attack as precipitating only loss is to see but half the picture. When Santiago says, "Fishing kills me exactly as it keeps me alive," he is pointing, once again, to the vast, necessary, and ever-shifting tension that exists between loss and gain, triumph and defeat, life and death.

In the final pages of the novella, Hemingway employs a number of images that link Santiago to Christ, the model of transcendence, who turned loss into gain, defeat into triumph, and even death into new life. Hemingway unabashedly paints the old man as a crucified martyr: as soon as the sharks arrive, the narrator comments that the noise Santiago made resembled the noise one would make "feeling the nail go through his hands and into the wood." The narrator's description of Santiago's return to town also recalls the crucifixion. As the old man struggles up the hill with his mast across his shoulders, the reader cannot help but recall Christ's march toward Calvary. Even the position in which he collapses on his bed—he sleeps facedown on the newspapers with his arms out straight and the palms of his hands up—brings to mind the image of Christ suffering on the cross.

IMPORTANT QUOTATIONS EXPLAINED

1.   He no longer dreamed of storms, nor of women, nor of
     great occurrences, nor of great fish, nor fights, nor contests
     of strength, nor of his wife. He only dreamed of places now
     and of the lions on the beach. They played like young cats
     in the dusk and he loved them as he loved the boy.

Since the publication of *The Old Man and the Sea,* there has been
much debate surrounding the story's symbols. Does the old man
represent the author nearing the end of his career? Do the vicious
sharks stand for cruel literary critics or the inevitably destructive
forces of nature? While most readers agree that, as a parable, *The
Old Man and the Sea* addresses universal life, the image of the lions playing on the African beach, which is presented three times in
the novel, remains something of an enigma. Like poetry, the lions
are supremely suggestive without being tethered to a single meaning. Indeed, the only certainty about the image is that it serves as a
source of comfort and renewal for Santiago.

This passage, which describes Santiago's dreams on the night
before he sets out for his fishing expedition (the first day that the
narrative covers), simultaneously confirms and moves beyond
Hemingway's immediately recognizable vision of the universe.
Hemingway made his career telling stories about "great occur-
rences," "great fish," and "contests of strength." The fact that Santiago no longer dreams of any of these makes him unique among
Hemingway's heroes. Of course, by dreaming of lions he is still in
a recognizably "Hemingwayesque" world, but the lions here are at
play and thus suggest a time of youth and ease. They are also linked
explicitly to Manolin, a connection that is made apparent at the end
of the novel as the boy watches over his aged friend as Santiago's
dream of the lions returns.

2.   Just then the stern line came taut under his foot, where he
       had kept the loop of the line, and he dropped his oars and
       felt the weight of the small tuna's shivering pull as he held
       the line firm and commenced to haul it in. The shivering
       increased as he pulled in and he could see the blue back
       of the fish in the water and the gold of his sides before
       he swung him over the side and into the boat. He lay in
       the stern in the sun, compact and bullet shaped, his big,
       unintelligent eyes staring as he thumped his life out against
       the planking of the boat with the quick shivering strokes of
       his neat, fast-moving tail. The old man hit him on the head
       for kindness and kicked him, his body still shuddering,
       under the shade of the stern.

This passage, which describes Santiago's hauling in of the tuna on
the second day of the narrative, exemplifies the power and beauty
of the simple, evocative style of prose that earned Hemingway his
reputation as a revolutionary and influenced generations of writers
to come. Hemingway's strength and mastery lies in his ability to render concrete but still poetic images using familiar words and simple
vocabulary. The scene above is instantly familiar, even to the many
readers who have no experience hauling in fish. For instance, the
"compact and bullet shaped" fish is remarkably visible as it shivers
and shudders on the floor of the skiff. Hemingway loads the passage
with carefully chosen sounds. For instance, the repetition of the "k"
and "s" sounds in the last sentence suggests a calm, rhythmic mo-
tion, like the breaking of waves against the boat or the side-to-side
twitching of the fish's body.

The passage also demonstrates the psychological depths Hemingway could access despite his incredible economy of language. When
the old man hits the fish on the head, Hemingway qualifies the action
with only two words: "for kindness." These two words, however,
give the reader full insight into the old man's character. Hemingway renders Santiago's connection to, and respect and love for, the
world in which he lives without reporting the old man's innermost
thoughts. Instead, using two well-chosen words, he hints at a depth
of feeling that makes Santiago who he is. Hemingway described
this technique as the "iceberg principle," for he believed that the
simplest writing, when done well, would hint at the greatest human
truths, just as the tip of an iceberg hinted at the terrific frozen mass
that rested underwater.

3.   "I have never seen or heard of such a fish. But I must kill him. I am glad we do not have to try to kill the stars." Imagine if each day a man must try to kill the moon, he thought. The moon runs away. . . . Then he was sorry for the great fish that had nothing to eat and his determination to kill him never relaxed in his sorrow for him. . . . There is no one worthy of eating him from the manner of his behavior and his great dignity. I do not understand these things, he thought. But it is good that we do not have to try to kill the sun or the moon or the stars. It is enough to live on the sea and kill our true brothers.

This passage is found at the end of the third day related by the novella. As Santiago struggles with the marlin, he reflects upon the nature of the universe and his place in it. He displays both pity for the fish and an unflagging determination to kill it, because the marlin's death helps to reinvigorate the fisherman's life. The predatory nature of this exchange is inevitable, for just as hawks will continue to hunt warblers, men will continue to kill marlin, and sharks will continue to rob them of their catches. The cruelty of this natural order is subverted, however, because of the kinship Santiago feels for his prey. His opponent is worthy—so worthy, in fact, that he later goes on to say that it doesn't matter who kills whom. There is, in the old man's estimation, some sense to this order. Man can achieve greatness only when placed in a well-matched contest against his earthly brothers. To find glory, Santiago does not need to extend himself beyond his animal nature by looking to the sun or the stars.

QUOTATIONS

4.   Then the fish came alive, with his death in him, and rose
      high out of the water showing all his great length and
      width and all his power and his beauty. He seemed to hang
      in the air above the old man in the skiff. Then he fell into
      the water with a crash that sent spray over the old man and
      over all of the skiff.

The killing of the marlin, which occurs on the fourth day of the
narrative, marks the climax of the novella. The end of the marlin's
life is the most vital of moments, as the fish comes alive "with his
death in him" and exhibits to Santiago, more strongly than ever
before, "all his power and his beauty." The fish seems to transcend
his own death, because it invests him with a new life. This notion of
transcendence is important, for it resounds within Santiago's story.
Like the fish, the old man suffers something of a death on his way
back to the village. He is stripped of his quarry and, given his age,
will likely never have the opportunity to land such a magnificent fish
again. Nevertheless, he returns to the village with his spirit and his
reputation revitalized.

QUOTATIONS

5. You did not kill the fish only to keep alive and to sell for
food, he thought. You killed him for pride and because you
are a fisherman. You loved him when he was alive and you
loved him after. If you love him, it is not a sin to kill him.
Or is it more?

As Santiago sails back to his village on the fourth day of the novella,
towing behind him the carcass of the decimated marlin, he tries
to make sense of the destruction he has witnessed. He feels deeply
apologetic toward the fish, which he sees as too dignified for such a
wasteful end. He attempts to explain to himself his reasons for killing the fish, and admits that his desire to hunt the fish stemmed from
the very same quality that led to its eventual destruction: his pride.
He then justifies his behavior by claiming that his slaying of the
marlin was necessitated by his love and respect for it. Indeed, when
Santiago kills the fish, the loss of life is somehow transcendently
beautiful, as opposed to the bold, senseless scavenging on the part
of the sharks.

KEY FACTS

FULL TITLE
The Old Man and the Sea

AUTHOR
Ernest Hemingway

TYPE OF WORK
Novella

GENRE
Parable; tragedy

LANGUAGE
English

TIME AND PLACE WRITTEN
1951, Cuba

DATE OF FIRST PUBLICATION
1952

PUBLISHER
Scribner's

NARRATOR
The novella is narrated by an anonymous narrator.

POINT OF VIEW
Sometimes the narrator describes the characters and events objectively, that is, as they would appear to an outside observer. However, the narrator frequently provides details about Santiago's inner thoughts and dreams.

TONE
Despite the narrator's journalistic, matter-of-fact tone, his reverence for Santiago and his struggle is apparent. The text affirms its hero to a degree unusual even for Hemingway.

TENSE
Past

SETTING (TIME)

Late 1940s

SETTING (PLACE)

A small fishing village near Havana, Cuba; the waters of the Gulf of Mexico

PROTAGONIST

Santiago

MAJOR CONFLICT

For three days, Santiago struggles against the greatest fish of his long career.

RISING ACTION

After eighty-four successive days without catching a fish, Santiago promises his former assistant, Manolin, that he will go "far out" into the ocean. The marlin takes the bait, but Santiago is unable to reel him in, which leads to a three-day struggle between the fisherman and the fish.

CLIMAX

The marlin circles the skiff while Santiago slowly reels him in. Santiago nearly passes out from exhaustion but gathers enough strength to harpoon the marlin through the heart, causing him to lurch in an almost sexual climax of vitality before dying.

FALLING ACTION

Santiago sails back to shore with the marlin tied to his boat. Sharks follow the marlin's trail of blood and destroy it. Santiago arrives home toting only the fish's skeletal carcass. The village fishermen respect their formerly ridiculed peer, and Manolin pledges to return to fishing with Santiago. Santiago falls into a deep sleep and dreams of lions.

THEMES

The honor in struggle, defeat, and death; pride as the source of greatness and determination

MOTIFS

Crucifixion imagery; life from death; the lions on the beach

SYMBOLS

The marlin; the shovel-nosed sharks

FORESHADOWING

Santiago's insistence that he will sail out farther than ever before foreshadows his destruction; because the marlin is linked to Santiago, the marlin's death foreshadows Santiago's own destruction by the sharks.

STUDY QUESTIONS

1.   *What is the role of the sea in* THE OLD MAN AND THE SEA?

The rich waters of the Gulf Stream provide a revolving cast of bit players—birds and beasts—that the old man observes and greets. Through Santiago's interactions with these figures, his character emerges. In fact, Santiago is so connected to these waters, which he thinks of good-humoredly as a sometimes fickle lover, that the sea acts almost like a lens through which the reader views his character. Santiago's interaction with the weary warbler, for instance, shows not only his kindness but also, as he thinks about the hawks that will inevitably hunt the tiny bird, a philosophy that dominates and structures his life. His strength, resolve, and pride are measured in terms of how far out into the gulf he sails. The sea also provides glimpses of the depth of Santiago's knowledge: in his comments about the wind, the current, and the friction of the water reside an entire lifetime of experience, skill, and dedication. When, at the end of the novella, Manolin states that he still has much to learn from the old man, it seems an expression of the obvious.

STUDY QUESTIONS

2. *Santiago is considered by many readers to be a tragic hero, in that his greatest strength—his pride—leads to his eventual downfall. Discuss the role of pride in Santiago's plight.*

At first, Santiago's plight seems rather hopeless. He has gone eighty-four days without catching a fish, and he is the laughingstock of his small village. Regardless of his past, the old man determines to change his luck and sail out farther than he or the other fishermen ever have before. His commitment to sailing out to where the big fish are testifies to the depth of his pride. Later, after the sharks have destroyed his prize marlin, Santiago chastises himself for his hubris, claiming that it has ruined both the marlin and himself. Yet, Santiago's pride also enables him to achieve what he otherwise would not. Not until he meets and battles the marlin are his skills as a fisherman truly put to the test. In other words, the pride that leads to the destruction of his quarry also helps him earn the deeper respect of the village fishermen and secures him the prized companionship of the boy.

STUDY QUESTIONS

THE OLD MAN AND THE SEA ❧ 45

3. *Discuss religious symbolism in* THE OLD MAN AND
   THE SEA. *To what effect does Hemingway employ such
   images?*

Christian symbolism, especially images that refer to the crucifixion
of Christ, is present throughout *The Old Man and the Sea*. During
the old man's battle with the marlin, his palms are cut by his fishing
cable. Given Santiago's suffering and willingness to sacrifice his
life, the wounds are suggestive of Christ's stigmata, and Hemingway goes on to portray the old man as a Christ-like martyr. As
soon as the sharks arrive, Santiago makes a noise one would make
"feeling the nail go through his hands and into the wood." And the
old man's struggle up the hill to his village with his mast across his
shoulders is evocative of Christ's march toward Calvary. Even the
position in which Santiago collapses on his bed—he lies face down
with his arms out straight and the palms of his hands up—brings
to mind the image of Christ on the cross. Hemingway employs
these images in order to link Santiago to Christ, who exemplified
transcendence by turning loss into gain, defeat into triumph, and
even death into life.

STUDY QUESTIONS

How to Write
Literary Analysis

The Literary Essay: A Step-by-Step Guide

When you read for pleasure, your only goal is enjoyment. You might find yourself reading to get caught up in an exciting story, to learn about an interesting time or place, or just to pass time. Maybe you're looking for inspiration, guidance, or a reflection of your own life. There are as many different, valid ways of reading a book as there are books in the world.

When you read a work of literature in an English class, however, you're being asked to read in a special way: you're being asked to perform *literary analysis*. To analyze something means to break it down into smaller parts and then examine how those parts work, both individually and together. Literary analysis involves examining all the parts of a novel, play, short story, or poem—elements such as character, setting, tone, and imagery—and thinking about how the author uses those elements to create certain effects.

A literary essay isn't a book review: you're not being asked whether or not you liked a book or whether you'd recommend it to another reader. A literary essay also isn't like the kind of book report you wrote when you were younger, where your teacher wanted you to summarize the book's action. A high school- or college-level literary essay asks, "How does this piece of literature actually work?" "How does it do what it does?" and, "Why might the author have made the choices he or she did?"

The Seven Steps
No one is born knowing how to analyze literature; it's a skill you learn and a process you can master. As you gain more practice with this kind of thinking and writing, you'll be able to craft a method that works best for you. But until then, here are seven basic steps to writing a well-constructed literary essay:

1. *Ask questions*
2. *Collect evidence*
3. *Construct a thesis*

4. *Develop and organize arguments*
5. *Write the introduction*
6. *Write the body paragraphs*
7. *Write the conclusion*

---

1. ASK QUESTIONS

When you're assigned a literary essay in class, your teacher will often provide you with a list of writing prompts. Lucky you! Now all you have to do is choose one. Do yourself a favor and pick a topic that interests you. You'll have a much better (not to mention easier) time if you start off with something you enjoy thinking about. If you are asked to come up with a topic by yourself, though, you might start to feel a little panicked. Maybe you have too many ideas—or none at all. Don't worry. Take a deep breath and start by asking yourself these questions:

- **What struck you?** Did a particular image, line, or scene linger in your mind for a long time? If it fascinated you, chances are you can draw on it to write a fascinating essay.

- **What confused you?** Maybe you were surprised to see a character act in a certain way, or maybe you didn't understand why the book ended the way it did. Confusing moments in a work of literature are like a loose thread in a sweater: if you pull on it, you can unravel the entire thing. Ask yourself why the author chose to write about that character or scene the way he or she did and you might tap into some important insights about the work as a whole.

- **Did you notice any patterns?** Is there a phrase that the main character uses constantly or an image that repeats throughout the book? If you can figure out how that pattern weaves through the work and what the significance of that pattern is, you've almost got your entire essay mapped out.

- **Did you notice any contradictions or ironies?** Great works of literature are complex; great literary essays recognize and explain those complexities. Maybe the title (*Happy Days*) totally disagrees with the book's subject matter (hungry orphans dying in the woods). Maybe the main character acts one way around his family and a completely different way around his friends and associates. If you can find a way to explain a work's contradictory elements, you've got the seeds of a great essay.

At this point, you don't need to know exactly what you're going to say about your topic; you just need a place to begin your exploration. You can help direct your reading and brainstorming by formulating your topic as a *question,* which you'll then try to answer in your essay. The best questions invite critical debates and discussions, not just a rehashing of the summary. Remember, you're looking for something you can *prove or argue* based on evidence you find in the text. Finally, remember to keep the scope of your question in mind: is this a topic you can adequately address within the word or page limit you've been given? Conversely, is this a topic big enough to fill the required length?

GOOD QUESTIONS

"Are Romeo and Juliet's parents responsible for the deaths of their children?"

"Why do pigs keep showing up in LORD OF THE FLIES*?"*

"Are Dr. Frankenstein and his monster alike? How?"

BAD QUESTIONS

"What happens to Scout in TO KILL A MOCKINGBIRD*?"*

"What do the other characters in JULIUS CAESAR *think about Caesar?"*

"How does Hester Prynne in THE SCARLET LETTER *remind me of my sister?"*

---

2. COLLECT EVIDENCE

Once you know what question you want to answer, it's time to scour the book for things that will help you answer the question. Don't worry if you don't know what you want to say yet—right now you're just collecting ideas and material and letting it all percolate. Keep track of passages, symbols, images, or scenes that deal with your topic. Eventually, you'll start making connections between these examples and your thesis will emerge.

Here's a brief summary of the various parts that compose each and every work of literature. These are the elements that you will analyze in your essay, and which you will offer as evidence to support your arguments. For more on the parts of literary works, see the Glossary of Literary Terms at the end of this section.

LITERARY ANALYSIS

ELEMENTS OF STORY   These are the *what*s of the work—what happens, where it happens, and to whom it happens.

- **Plot:** All of the events and actions of the work.

- **Character:** The people who act and are acted upon in a literary work. The main character of a work is known as the *protagonist*.

- **Conflict:** The central tension in the work. In most cases, the protagonist wants something, while opposing forces (antagonists) hinder the protagonist's progress.

- **Setting:** When and where the work takes place. Elements of setting include location, time period, time of day, weather, social atmosphere, and economic conditions.

- **Narrator:** The person telling the story. The narrator may straightforwardly report what happens, convey the subjective opinions and perceptions of one or more characters, or provide commentary and opinion in his or her own voice.

- **Themes:** The main idea or message of the work—usually an abstract idea about people, society, or life in general. A work may have many themes, which may be in tension with one another.

ELEMENTS OF STYLE   These are the *how*s—how the characters speak, how the story is constructed, and how language is used throughout the work.

- **Structure and organization:** How the parts of the work are assembled. Some novels are narrated in a linear, chronological fashion, while others skip around in time. Some plays follow a traditional three- or five-act structure, while others are a series of loosely connected scenes. Some authors deliberately leave gaps in their works, leaving readers to puzzle out the missing information. A work's structure and organization can tell you a lot about the kind of message it wants to convey.

- **Point of view:** The perspective from which a story is told. In *first-person point of view,* the narrator involves him or herself in the story. ("I went to the store"; "We watched in horror as the bird slammed into the window.") A first-person narrator is usually the protagonist of the work, but not always. In *third-person point of view,* the narrator does not participate

LITERARY ANALYSIS

in the story. A third-person narrator may closely follow a specific character, recounting that individual character's thoughts or experiences, or it may be what we call an *omniscient* narrator. Omniscient narrators see and know all: they can witness any event in any time or place and are privy to the inner thoughts and feelings of all characters. Remember that the narrator and the author are not the same thing!

- **Diction:** Word choice. Whether a character uses dry, clinical language or flowery prose with lots of exclamation points can tell you a lot about his or her attitude and personality.

- **Syntax:** Word order and sentence construction. Syntax is a crucial part of establishing an author's narrative voice. Ernest Hemingway, for example, is known for writing in very short, straightforward sentences, while James Joyce characteristically wrote in long, incredibly complicated lines.

- **Tone:** The mood or feeling of the text. Diction and syntax often contribute to the tone of a work. A novel written in short, clipped sentences that use small, simple words might feel brusque, cold, or matter-of-fact.

- **Imagery:** Language that appeals to the senses, representing things that can be seen, smelled, heard, tasted, or touched.

- **Figurative language:** Language that is not meant to be interpreted literally. The most common types of figurative language are *metaphors* and *similes,* which compare two unlike things in order to suggest a similarity between them— for example, "All the world's a stage," or "The moon is like a ball of green cheese." (Metaphors say one thing *is* another thing; similes claim that one thing is *like* another thing.)

---

3. CONSTRUCT A THESIS

When you've examined all the evidence you've collected and know how you want to answer the question, it's time to write your thesis statement. A *thesis* is a claim about a work of literature that needs to be supported by evidence and arguments. The thesis statement is the heart of the literary essay, and the bulk of your paper will be spent trying to prove this claim. A good thesis will be:

- **Arguable.** "*The Great Gatsby* describes New York society in the 1920s" isn't a thesis—it's a fact.

- **Provable through textual evidence**. "*Hamlet* is a confusing but ultimately very well-written play" is a weak thesis because it offers the writer's personal opinion about the book. Yes, it's arguable, but it's not a claim that can be proved or supported with examples taken from the play itself.

- **Surprising**. "Both George and Lenny change a great deal in *Of Mice and Men*" is a weak thesis because it's obvious. A really strong thesis will argue for a reading of the text that is not immediately apparent.

- **Specific**. "Dr. Frankenstein's monster tells us a lot about the human condition" is *almost* a really great thesis statement, but it's still too vague. What does the writer mean by "a lot"? *How* does the monster tell us so much about the human condition?

GOOD THESIS STATEMENTS

Question: In *Romeo and Juliet*, which is more powerful in shaping the lovers' story: fate or foolishness?

Thesis: "Though Shakespeare defines Romeo and Juliet as 'star-crossed lovers' and images of stars and planets appear throughout the play, a closer examination of that celestial imagery reveals that the stars are merely witnesses to the characters' foolish activities and not the causes themselves."

Question: How does the bell jar function as a symbol in Sylvia Plath's *The Bell Jar*?

Thesis: "A bell jar is a bell-shaped glass that has three basic uses: to hold a specimen for observation, to contain gases, and to maintain a vacuum. The bell jar appears in each of these capacities in *The Bell Jar*, Plath's semi-autobiographical novel, and each appearance marks a different stage in Esther's mental breakdown."

Question: Would Piggy in *The Lord of the Flies* make a good island leader if he were given the chance?

Thesis: "Though the intelligent, rational, and innovative Piggy has the mental characteristics of a good leader, he ultimately lacks the social skills necessary to be an effective one. Golding emphasizes this point by giving Piggy a foil in the charismatic Jack, whose magnetic personality allows him to capture and wield power effectively, if not always wisely."

LITERARY ANALYSIS

4. DEVELOP AND ORGANIZE ARGUMENTS

The reasons and examples that support your thesis will form the middle paragraphs of your essay. Since you can't really write your thesis statement until you know how you'll structure your argument, you'll probably end up working on steps 3 and 4 at the same time.

There's no single method of argumentation that will work in every context. One essay prompt might ask you to compare and contrast two characters, while another asks you to trace an image through a given work of literature. These questions require different kinds of answers and therefore different kinds of arguments. Below, we'll discuss three common kinds of essay prompts and some strategies for constructing a solid, well-argued case.

TYPES OF LITERARY ESSAYS

- **Compare and contrast**

   Compare and contrast the characters of Huck and Jim in THE ADVENTURES OF HUCKLEBERRY FINN.

   Chances are you've written this kind of essay before. In an academic literary context, you'll organize your arguments the same way you would in any other class. You can either go *subject by subject* or *point by point*. In the former, you'll discuss one character first and then the second. In the latter, you'll choose several traits (attitude toward life, social status, images and metaphors associated with the character) and devote a paragraph to each. You may want to use a mix of these two approaches—for example, you may want to spend a paragraph a piece broadly sketching Huck's and Jim's personalities before transitioning into a paragraph or two that describes a few key points of comparison. This can be a highly effective strategy if you want to make a counterintuitive argument—that, despite seeming to be totally different, the two objects being compared are actually similar in a very important way (or vice versa). Remember that your essay should reveal something fresh or unexpected about the text, so think beyond the obvious parallels and differences.

- **Trace**

   Choose an image—for example, birds, knives, or eyes—and trace that image throughout MACBETH.

   Sounds pretty easy, right? All you need to do is read the play, underline every appearance of a knife in *Macbeth*, and then list them in your essay in the order they appear, right? Well, not exactly. Your teacher doesn't want a simple catalog of examples. He or she wants to see you make *connections* between those examples—that's the difference between summarizing and analyzing. In the *Macbeth* example above, think about the different contexts in which knives appear in the play and to what effect. In *Macbeth*, there are real knives and imagined knives; knives that kill and knives that simply threaten. Categorize and classify your examples to give them some order. Finally, always keep the overall effect in mind. After you choose and analyze your examples, you should come to some greater understanding about the work, as well as your chosen image, symbol, or phrase's role in developing the major themes and stylistic strategies of that work.

- **Debate**

    Is the society depicted in 1984 *good for its citizens?*

    In this kind of essay, you're being asked to debate a moral, ethical, or aesthetic issue regarding the work. You might be asked to judge a character or group of characters (*Is Caesar responsible for his own demise?*) or the work itself (*Is* JANE EYRE *a feminist novel?*). For this kind of essay, there are two important points to keep in mind. First, don't simply base your arguments on your personal feelings and reactions. Every literary essay expects you to read and analyze the work, so search for evidence in the text. What do characters in *1984* have to say about the government of Oceania? What images does Orwell use that might give you a hint about his attitude toward the government? As in any debate, you also need to make sure that you define all the necessary terms before you begin to argue your case. What does it mean to be a "good" society? What makes a novel "feminist"? You should define your terms right up front, in the first paragraph after your introduction.

    Second, remember that strong literary essays make contrary and surprising arguments. Try to think outside the box. In the *1984* example above, it seems like the obvious answer would be no, the totalitarian society depicted in Orwell's novel is *not* good for its citizens. But can you think of any arguments for the opposite side? Even if your final assertion is that the novel depicts a cruel, repressive, and therefore harmful society, acknowledging and responding to the counterargument will strengthen your overall case.

LITERARY ANALYSIS

5. WRITE THE INTRODUCTION

Your introduction sets up the entire essay. It's where you present your topic and articulate the particular issues and questions you'll be addressing. It's also where you, as the writer, introduce yourself to your readers. A persuasive literary essay immediately establishes its writer as a knowledgeable, authoritative figure.

An introduction can vary in length depending on the overall length of the essay, but in a traditional five-paragraph essay it should be no longer than one paragraph. However long it is, your introduction needs to:

- **Provide any necessary context.** Your introduction should situate the reader and let him or her know what to expect. What book are you discussing? Which characters? What topic will you be addressing?

- **Answer the "So what?" question.** Why is this topic important, and why is your particular position on the topic noteworthy? Ideally, your introduction should pique the reader's interest by suggesting how your argument is surprising or otherwise counterintuitive. Literary essays make unexpected connections and reveal less-than-obvious truths.

- **Present your thesis.** This usually happens at or very near the end of your introduction.

- **Indicate the shape of the essay to come.** Your reader should finish reading your introduction with a good sense of the scope of your essay as well as the path you'll take toward proving your thesis. You don't need to spell out every step, but you do need to suggest the organizational pattern you'll be using.

Your introduction should not:

- **Be vague.** Beware of the two killer words in literary analysis: *interesting* and *important*. Of course the work, question, or example is interesting and important—that's why you're writing about it!

- **Open with any grandiose assertions.** Many student readers think that beginning their essays with a flamboyant statement such as, "Since the dawn of time, writers have been fascinated with the topic of free will," makes them sound important and commanding. You know what? It actually sounds pretty amateurish.

- **Wildly praise the work.** Another typical mistake student writers make is extolling the work or author. Your teacher doesn't need to be told that "Shakespeare is perhaps the greatest writer in the English language." You can mention a work's reputation in passing—by referring to *The Adventures of Huckleberry Finn* as "Mark Twain's enduring classic," for example—but don't make a point of bringing it up unless that reputation is key to your argument.

- **Go off-topic.** Keep your introduction streamlined and to the point. Don't feel the need to throw in all kinds of bells and whistles in order to impress your reader—just get to the point as quickly as you can, without skimping on any of the required steps.

6. Write the Body Paragraphs

Once you've written your introduction, you'll take the arguments you developed in step 4 and turn them into your body paragraphs. The organization of this middle section of your essay will largely be determined by the argumentative strategy you use, but no matter how you arrange your thoughts, your body paragraphs need to do the following:

- **Begin with a strong topic sentence.** Topic sentences are like signs on a highway: they tell the reader where they are and where they're going. A good topic sentence not only alerts readers to what issue will be discussed in the following paragraph but also gives them a sense of what argument will be made *about* that issue. "Rumor and gossip play an important role in *The Crucible*" isn't a strong topic sentence because it doesn't tell us very much. "The community's constant gossiping creates an environment that allows false accusations to flourish" is a much stronger topic sentence— it not only tells us *what* the paragraph will discuss (gossip) but *how* the paragraph will discuss the topic (by showing how gossip creates a set of conditions that leads to the play's climactic action).

- **Fully and completely develop a single thought.** Don't skip around in your paragraph or try to stuff in too much material. Body paragraphs are like bricks: each individual

LITERARY ANALYSIS

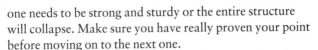

one needs to be strong and sturdy or the entire structure will collapse. Make sure you have really proven your point before moving on to the next one.

- **Use transitions effectively.** Good literary essay writers know that each paragraph must be clearly and strongly linked to the material around it. Think of each paragraph as a response to the one that precedes it. Use transition words and phrases such as *however, similarly, on the contrary, therefore,* and *furthermore* to indicate what kind of response you're making.

---

7. Write the Conclusion

Just as you used the introduction to ground your readers in the topic before providing your thesis, you'll use the conclusion to quickly summarize the specifics learned thus far and then hint at the broader implications of your topic. A good conclusion will:

- **Do more than simply restate the thesis.** If your thesis argued that *The Catcher in the Rye* can be read as a Christian allegory, don't simply end your essay by saying, "And that is why *The Catcher in the Rye* can be read as a Christian allegory." If you've constructed your arguments well, this kind of statement will just be redundant.

- **Synthesize the arguments, not summarize them.** Similarly, don't repeat the details of your body paragraphs in your conclusion. The reader has already read your essay, and chances are it's not so long that they've forgotten all your points by now.

- **Revisit the "So what?" question.** In your introduction, you made a case for why your topic and position are important. You should close your essay with the same sort of gesture. What do your readers know now that they didn't know before? How will that knowledge help them better appreciate or understand the work overall?

- **Move from the specific to the general.** Your essay has most likely treated a very specific element of the work—a single character, a small set of images, or a particular passage. In your conclusion, try to show how this narrow discussion has wider implications for the work overall. If your essay on *To Kill a Mockingbird* focused on the character of Boo Radley, for example, you might want to include a bit in your conclusion about how he fits into the novel's larger message about childhood, innocence, or family life.

- **Stay relevant.** Your conclusion should suggest new directions of thought, but it shouldn't be treated as an opportunity to pad your essay with all the extra, interesting ideas you came up with during your brainstorming sessions but couldn't fit into the essay proper. Don't attempt to stuff in unrelated queries or too many abstract thoughts.

- **Avoid making overblown closing statements.** A conclusion should open up your highly specific, focused discussion, but it should do so without drawing a sweeping lesson about life or human nature. Making such observations may be part of the point of reading, but it's almost always a mistake in essays, where these observations tend to sound overly dramatic or simply silly.

A+ ESSAY CHECKLIST

Congratulations! If you've followed all the steps we've outlined above, you should have a solid literary essay to show for all your efforts. What if you've got your sights set on an A+? To write the kind of superlative essay that will be rewarded with a perfect grade, keep the following rubric in mind. These are the qualities that teachers expect to see in a truly A+ essay. How does yours stack up?

- ✓ Demonstrates a thorough understanding of the book
- ✓ Presents an original, compelling argument
- ✓ Thoughtfully analyzes the text's formal elements
- ✓ Uses appropriate and insightful examples
- ✓ Structures ideas in a logical and progressive order
- ✓ Demonstrates a mastery of sentence construction, transitions, grammar, spelling, and word choice

Suggested Essay Topics

1. *Discuss Hemingway's "iceberg" principle of writing in relation to* The Old Man and the Sea.

2. *What significance do the lions on the beach have for the old man?*

3. *"A man can be destroyed but not defeated," says the old man after the first shark attack. At the end of the story, is the old man defeated? Why or why not?*

4. The Old Man and the Sea *is, essentially, the story of a single character. Indeed, other than the old man, only one human being receives any kind of prolonged attention. Discuss the role of Manolin in the novella. Is he necessary to the book?*

A+ Student Essay

Ernest Hemingway's *The Old Man and the Sea* contains
Christian themes and imagery. Should it be considered a
Christian novel?

The Old Man and the Sea resembles a Christian parable in many
ways. Its protagonist, the fisherman Santiago, seems to exemplify
Christian virtues, and the narrative clearly and repeatedly connects
his trials at sea to Christ's suffering on the cross. However, a careful
examination of Santiago's character and actions shows that he is
not a Christian character and that, in reality, he embodies a warrior ethic that is incompatible with Christian ideals. The parallels
between *The Old Man and the Sea* and the familiar Biblical story
of the crucifixion add narrative and emotional power to the novel,
but Hemingway does not use them to advance a religious moral or
lesson. Instead, they serve to advance Santiago's warrior philosophy. Though *The Old Man and the Sea* has superficial Christian
elements, at its core it cannot be considered a Christian novel.

Initially, Santiago seems to be an ideal Christian. He keeps Christian icons in his house, he refers to God and Christ repeatedly, and
Hemingway calls attention to his "faith," "hope," and "love"—the
three principal Christian virtues. However, these appearances are
superficial. For example, though Santiago says he has "faith," he
doesn't use the word in a religious sense; rather, he uses it in connection with a superstitious idea of luck and to describe his feelings
about baseball. When he prays during his battle with the fish, he
prefaces his prayers by saying he is not religious and then proceeds
to recite them mechanically, forgetting the words. Santiago's careful and disciplined approach to everything in life is emphasized
throughout the novel, so his sloppiness here only draws attention
to his lack of commitment to his prayers. Even more important,
Santiago never thinks of God. Instead, he finds comfort, strength,
and meaning by thinking of secular things: the human world, baseball, and the creatures of the sea—not religion.

Santiago is not religious, but he does live by a moral code and
has a philosophy of life. He is a master of his craft, much more
attentive to its fine details than the other fisherman in his village are.
He exemplifies the manly virtues of courage and determination. In
addition, he has a strong sense of right and wrong when it comes to

LITERARY ANALYSIS

killing. He loves and respects the fish he pursues, considering them his "brothers," and he abhors killing a creature for no good purpose. More than anything else, Santiago has an enduring pride, which he expresses most clearly in the moments he realizes that more sharks are coming to eat the great marlin he has caught. He says, "A man can be destroyed but not defeated"—that is, a true man will fight to the bitter end, to death if needed, but he will never give up. Together, these principles form a fiercely independent warrior's philosophy of life, where living well is about meeting adversaries in honorable battle. This is not a Christian outlook on life, which would advocate a patient forbearance and a meek tolerance of hardship.

Ironically, Hemingway uses Christian symbolism to advance this alternate worldview. After Santiago has hooked the great marlin, he passes the fishing line across his back and holds it in both hands, cutting his palms repeatedly. This posture resembles that of Christ on the cross, and Santiago's wounds evoke the stigmata, the puncture wounds Christ bore from the crucifixion. But at the end of his suffering, Santiago is not redeemed or reborn like Christ. Rather, his fish is stolen from him by sharks, and he returns to land close to death. His suffering can only be considered redemptive because, in Santiago's view, struggle and forbearance are ends in themselves. In the novel's philosophy, we are our best and truest selves only in a death struggle. This message is best illustrated in Hemingway's description of the very moment of the fish's death: "Then the fish came alive, with his death in him, and rose high out of the water showing all his great length and width and all his power and his beauty." Only in death does the fish come completely alive, or is its greatness entirely visible.

In a Christian parable, a deep religious message might be communicated through the actions of an ordinary man. In *The Old Man and the Sea*, Hemingway turns this literary convention on end. Instead, he appropriates the powerful, resonant story of Christ's crucifixion in order to convey and glorify the life philosophy of an ordinary man.

GLOSSARY OF LITERARY TERMS

ANTAGONIST
The entity that acts to frustrate the goals of the *protagonist*. The antagonist is usually another *character* but may also be a non-human force.

ANTIHERO / ANTIHEROINE
A *protagonist* who is not admirable or who challenges notions of what should be considered admirable.

CHARACTER
A person, animal, or any other thing with a personality that appears in a *narrative*.

CLIMAX
The moment of greatest intensity in a text or the major turning point in the *plot*.

CONFLICT
The central struggle that moves the *plot* forward. The conflict can be the *protagonist*'s struggle against fate, nature, society, or another person.

FIRST-PERSON POINT OF VIEW
A literary style in which the *narrator* tells the story from his or her own *point of view* and refers to himself or herself as "I." The narrator may be an active participant in the story or just an observer.

HERO / HEROINE
The principal *character* in a literary work or *narrative*.

IMAGERY
Language that brings to mind sense-impressions, representing things that can be seen, smelled, heard, tasted, or touched.

MOTIF
A recurring idea, structure, contrast, or device that develops or informs the major *themes* of a work of literature.

NARRATIVE
A story.

NARRATOR

The person (sometimes a *character*) who tells a story; the *voice* assumed by the writer. The narrator and the author of the work of literature are not the same person.

PLOT

The arrangement of the events in a story, including the sequence in which they are told, the relative emphasis they are given, and the causal connections between events.

POINT OF VIEW

The *perspective* that a *narrative* takes toward the events it describes.

PROTAGONIST

The main *character* around whom the story revolves.

SETTING

The location of a *narrative* in time and space. Setting creates mood or atmosphere.

SUBPLOT

A secondary *plot* that is of less importance to the overall story but may serve as a point of contrast or comparison to the main plot.

SYMBOL

An object, *character,* figure, or color that is used to represent an abstract idea or concept. Unlike an *emblem,* a symbol may have different meanings in different contexts.

SYNTAX

The way the words in a piece of writing are put together to form lines, phrases, or clauses; the basic structure of a piece of writing.

THEME

A fundamental and universal idea explored in a literary work.

TONE

The author's attitude toward the subject or *characters* of a story or poem or toward the reader.

VOICE

An author's individual way of using language to reflect his or her own personality and attitudes. An author communicates voice through *tone, diction,* and *syntax.*

LITERARY ANALYSIS

A Note on Plagiarism

Plagiarism—presenting someone else's work as your own—rears its ugly head in many forms. Many students know that copying text without citing it is unacceptable. But some don't realize that even if you're not quoting directly, but instead are paraphrasing or summarizing, *it is plagiarism* unless you cite the source.

Here are the most common forms of plagiarism:

- Using an author's phrases, sentences, or paragraphs without citing the source
- Paraphrasing an author's ideas without citing the source
- Passing off another student's work as your own

How do you steer clear of plagiarism? You should *always* acknowledge all words and ideas that aren't your own by using quotation marks around verbatim text or citations like footnotes and endnotes to note another writer's ideas. For more information on how to give credit when credit is due, ask your teacher for guidance or visit www.sparknotes.com.

Review & Resources

Quiz

1. When the novella opens, how long has it been since Santiago last caught a fish?

    A. 40 days
    B. 84 days
    C. 87 days
    D. 120 days

2. Manolin's parents refuse to let the boy fish with the old man because they believe Santiago is *salao*. How does Hemingway translate this word?

    A. "Crazy"
    B. "Selfish"
    C. "Washed up"
    D. "The worst form of unlucky"

3. How does Hemingway describe Santiago's eyes?

    A. They are full of pain.
    B. They are blank with defeat.
    C. They betray the weariness of his soul.
    D. They are the color of the sea.

4. What kind of reception does Santiago receive at the terrace café?

    A. The fishermen regard him as a hero.
    B. Most of the fishermen mock him.
    C. The successful fishermen offer him a portion of their day's catch.
    D. The younger fishermen pretend that the old man doesn't exist.

5. Who is Santiago's hero?

   A. Harry Truman
   B. Joe DiMaggio
   C. Dick Sisler
   D. Fidel Castro

6. What hangs on the wall of the old man's shack?

   A. A photograph of his wife
   B. The latest baseball scores
   C. A mounted fish
   D. Pictures

7. On the night before he promises Manolin to go "far out" to sea, of what does Santiago dream?

   A. A great storm
   B. A beautiful woman
   C. Lions on the beach
   D. A wrestling match

8. Why does Santiago not let his lines drift like the other fishermen?

   A. He is a stubborn man who prefers the old-fashioned way of fishing.
   B. He believes it is imprecise, and he strives always to be exact.
   C. It is dangerous, as he might become tangled with another boat.
   D. He is no longer young or strong enough to control a drifting line.

9. What kind of fish does Santiago first catch?

   A. A tuna
   B. A marlin
   C. A shrimp
   D. A Portuguese man-of-war

10. How does the old man know immediately the size of the great marlin he has caught?

   A. Soon after taking the bait, the fish jumps into the air, showing itself to the old man.
   B. Santiago has encountered this fish before as a younger man.
   C. He pulls and pulls on the line and nothing happens.
   D. He doesn't know the size of the fish until after the sharks have attacked it.

11. During his great struggle with the marlin, what does Santiago wish repeatedly?

   A. He wishes he were younger.
   B. He wishes for better equipment.
   C. He wishes that the fishermen who mocked him earlier were present to witness his victory.
   D. He wishes that the boy, Manolin, were with him.

12. In what year was *The Old Man and the Sea* published?

   A. 1950
   B. 1951
   C. 1952
   D. 1953

13. As his first full day of fighting with the fish wears on, what does Santiago begin to think about his adversary?

   A. He praises the fish because it promises to bring a wonderful price at market.
   B. He considers that he and the marlin are brothers, joined by the fact that they both ventured far out beyond all people and dangers in the water.
   C. He detests the fish for its vigor and vitality.
   D. He believes that the fish is a test of his worth, sent to him by God.

14. What does the weary warbler that lands on Santiago's fishing line make the old man think of?

    A. The probability that he, like the bird, will never make it back to land
    B. The predatory hawks that await the bird's arrival near land
    C. The hidden strength of the weak
    D. The beauty of the natural world

15. What happens to make Santiago curse the treachery of his own body?

    A. He gets seasick.
    B. He has diarrhea.
    C. His hand cramps.
    D. He needs to sleep.

16. In order to help himself catch the fish, what does Santiago do?

    A. He promises to pay more attention to Manolin upon his return.
    B. He decides to recite ten Hail Marys and ten Our Fathers.
    C. He lightens the boat by throwing all unnecessary weight overboard.
    D. He ties the skiff to a buoy so that the fish cannot pull it farther out to sea.

17. The great Joe DiMaggio suffers from what affliction?

    A. A bone spur
    B. Alcoholism
    C. A ruined knee
    D. Failing eyesight

18. To give himself confidence, Santiago remembers his contest with "the great negro of Cienfuegos." At what sport did the old man beat this challenger?

   A. Fencing
   B. Tennis
   C. Arm wrestling
   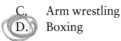 D. Boxing

19. Why does the thought of selling the fish's meat disappoint the old man?

   A. He knows people will cook the marlin, but it is best eaten raw.
   B. Market prices are low, and Santiago will get only a fraction of what the fish is worth.
   C. Because marlin has an unpleasant taste, Santiago wishes he caught something that made for better eating, like a shark.
   D. The people who will eat the meat are unworthy.

20. What does the old man remove and eat from the belly of a dolphin?

   A. Shrimp
   B. Flying fish
   C. Seaweed
   D. Piranha

21. How does Santiago finally kill the marlin?

   A. He harpoons it through the heart.
   B. He stabs it between the eyes.
   C. He lashes it to the inside of the boat.
   D. He bashes its head with his club.

22. How long does it take for the sharks to arrive and attack the marlin?

   A. Ten minutes
   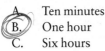 B. One hour
   C. Six hours
   D. A full day

23. After the shark attack, Santiago reflects that destruction is inevitable. How does he articulate this philosophy?

    A. The world is such an inhospitable place that no death should be mourned.
    B. Out, out, brief candle!
    C. Even the worthiest opponents must fall.
    D. Everything in the world kills everything else in some way.

24. What happens upon the old man's return to his fishing village?

    A. Manolin promises to sail with him.
    B. The fishermen mock Santiago for the folly of sailing out so far.
    C. Tourists ask the old man to recount his adventures.
    D. A statue is erected in his honor.

25. The old man remembers that once, when he killed a female marlin, the male marlin

    A. Bit the tail off the female
    B. Returned with a posse of marlins seeking revenge
    C. Made a sound like there were nails being driven through his fins
    D. Swam alongside the boat as though in mourning

REVIEW & RESOURCES

ANSWER KEY

1: B; 2: D; 3: D; 4: B; 5: B; 6: D; 7: C; 8: B; 9: A; 10: C; 11: D; 12: C;
13: B; 14: B; 15: C; 16: B; 17: A; 18: A; 19: C; 20: B; 21: A; 22: B;
23: D; 24: A; 25: D

Suggestions for Further Reading

BAKER, CARLOS. *Hemingway: The Writer as Artist*. Princeton, NJ: Princeton University Press, 1972.

BRENNER, GERRY. THE OLD MAN AND THE SEA: *Story of a Common Man*. Boston: Twayne Publishers, 1991.

HURLEY, C. HAROLD, ed. *Hemingway's Debt to Baseball in* THE OLD MAN AND THE SEA: *A Collection of Critical Readings*. Lewiston, NY: E. Mellen Press, 1992.

———. "Just 'a Boy' or 'Already a Man'?: Manolin's Age in *The Old Man and the Sea*," *The Hemingway Review* 10, no. 2. 95–101.

JOBES, KATHARINE T., comp. *Twentieth-Century Interpretations of* THE OLD MAN AND THE SEA: *A Collection of Critical Essays*. Englewood Cliffs, NJ: Prentice-Hall, 1968.

MORTON, BRUCE. "Santiago's Apprenticeship: A Source for *The Old Man and the Sea*," *The Hemingway Review* 2, no. 2. 52–55.

REYNOLDS, MICHAEL S. *Hemingway*. 5 vols. New York: W. W. Norton, 1998–2000.

WALDMEIR, JOSEPH J. and FREDERICK J. SVOBODA, eds. *Hemingway: Up in Michigan Perspectives*. East Lansing, MI: Michigan State University Press, 1995.

WEEKS, ROBERT P. *Hemingway: A Collection of Critical Essays*. Englewood Cliffs, NJ: Prentice-Hall, 1962.

YOUNG, PHILIP. *Ernest Hemingway*. Minneapolis: University of Minnesota Press, 1961.